Slovenly Love

Slovenly Love
Méira Cook

Brick Books

National Library of Canada Cataloguing in Publication

Cook, Méira, 1964-
        Slovenly love / Méira Cook.

Poems.
ISBN 1-894078-32-2
        I. Title.

PS8555.O567S56 2003   C811'.54   C2003-903697-9

We acknowledge the support of the Canada Council for the Arts, the Government of Canada through the Book Publishing Industry Development Program (BPIDP), and the Ontario Arts Council for their support of our publishing program.

The cover is after a photograph by the author. Robert Doisneau's photograph "Le baiser de l'hôtel de ville", (©Estate of Robert Dolisneau) is used courtesy of Agence Rapho.

The book is set in Sabon, Lublin Graph.

Design and layout by Alan Siu.

Printed and bound by Sunville Printco Inc.

Brick Books
431 Boler Road, Box 20081
London, Ontario   N6K 4G6
brick.books@sympatico.ca

for Shoshana

CONTENTS

A Year of Birds

Little bird you flutter-flutter in my arms, tick
thick milk and blood, cheeks
flying red flags where the unsheathed teeth
live. Outside geese scatter across sky,

iron filings thickening at the magnetic line
of horizon. This moment won't recur,
a sky rubbed thin
beneath the barefoot feet

of last summer's children. The window
is a frame stretching that paper-thin sky
along the bias of geese prejudiced
by weather. Little bird your unfinished head

crooks my arm, keeps my heart
coniferous. Even the horizon
exerts no pull. Instead a need
to bear witness. Like the man

on a bridge who sees the first
of the summer raptors, who calls
to the woman pushing her stroller below,
look up, *up!* Tilts her head, observes

their windpocked feathers, his mouth
spread in the shape of the word *eagle*
swooping towards her on the wind.
                                    As for me,

little bird, I am no longer hollow
boned, audacious. Gravity
keeps me buoyant, bright
anklet of teeth about the bone.

In the dark I hear little eyes
fly open, the glazed
where am I? of your stare louder
than wails that peel from your curly

mouth, shavings
off the narrow wedge of my sleep. Don't cry
little bird, honey-girl, sweet-and-bright.
                                    Listen you,

I will work the stars loose
from their clasps, I will
douse that good-night moon
dares blah-blah in your too-big

but-you'll-grow-into-them ears. Here's
the thing: I am not so young nor so prone
to metamorphoses as once I was. Joints
need oil something dreadful, skin too tight

stuffed sausage-full with unrequited
sleep. (An elegant Greek epigram
escapes me, lees
of wine staining the wineskin

would do for my breasts
if I could remember.) Compose
yourself baby, I say, but you turn
bird, flap the corners of the room

to panic and tussle, pinfeathers
whirling. In the morning,
thin drifts of word, the letter
V for good-bye in the sky.

What can you be smiling at in your sleep?
Milk, the crook of our arms. The la-la-la
tongue running across bare gum,
popped thumb, bowl of spoon. Broken

veins of sky behind my eyes. The colour
blue for which you have no name. A new
song to do with buses and wheels
you hated at first, being fretful

of anatomy, end rhymes, the transit
system for all I know. I know
all about incorrigible wheels, little spokes
dividing sunlight into wedges. The sweet

round of sleep curves the bow
of your lips, slips
between the uncut pages your mother
thumbs her way out of, losing

her place in the night's inflection. The metaphor
no substitute for what it replaces: sleep
spilling like milk over which
she has been cautioned not to cry, and night

slipping its stitches, unravelling
the soft knitted toy in her head.
How she hovers above the parenthesis
of your smile, casting off.

Your smile, baby, is a rind
protects the sweetest, most tender
flesh. Hush-puppy suede
your tongue, crisp

apple-crunch your cheek. Smile,
baby, at the tickle of word
growing to seed pearl and pout
in your oysterish mouth.

Two kinds of smiling: with teeth,
without. Yours a strawberry
compromise of gum and tooth pick-
picking your way from the egg. Half

a moon, Cheshire-girl, split to melon
with mirth at that yolk-eyed
marauding boy-baby, his
peach-cleft chin, his grin. Bodes well

for a future where agreement is the hinge
between upper and lower jaw, resistance
what takes up the slack of lip and cringe,
and smiling, baby, is the difference between.

Baby scat along
with Ella and me, sweet
heart, swee-tart sweet
and low. Oh-oh, over

and over we go. Hmmm-hmm.
Percussion-baby kicking out of time
to internal rhyme of pulse, breath,
your heart a jazz line spiked

between doo-be-doo and do-re
me and you. White notes, black
keys, everything contrary-wise
and left-handed (but that's the way

it crumbles, cookie-wise
and pound-foolish.) Or dark, dark
as teeth in photo negative. Days
hamstrung and out-of-joint, cumulus

gathering to a point of exasperation,
and nights shuffled between stiff fingers
like a deck of cards coming up red red red
as the Queen of Spades. Swing it girl,

like Ella an' Louis, unfurl. Teach
me, knot by knot, to loosen
the throat's slow noose. Here
we go then, baby! Un-re-hearsed —

Sleep is a thin crust these days,
easily broken. I dangle
feathers to your nose, angle a mirror.
Baby's breath soft as *gypsophila*

opens pink buds in your cheeks, sweet
joy befall thee. Me I fall
diagonally across sheets mumbling
felled, fallen, fallow. Gardens

weaving with drunken bees, bell
jasmine striking a sudden
white chord of memory, open
green wings in the narrow span

of pelvis, ribcage. Imagine a mouth
regenerating itself overnight,
effortlessly putting out mushrooms,
tulips, umbrellas. Better cut

the roses from my throat, withdraw
from metaphor before you turn
dandelion-hearted, blow
clockwise against the season. Fall

like rain like night like pride.
Turn dry as a leaf and rattle
through winter trees, the branches
of my arms.

Slowdown and sleepnow,
little hummingbird, wings
thrumming the air electric,
hair static with obstinacy.

Gravity is strong tonight, makes
falling in love easy. Rain strums
watery chords, turquoise
piano music slants steep

in eve of sky. We are all
fish swimming in circles
darting at words shining
like scale in water. Little

you, little v rhymes with me,
little w, double you, that's two of us
or we. Little x for kisses on your
little wise zed (that's head). Hmmm-

hmmm. Dreams pucker
that sleep-sticky mouth, hover
overhead, puffing steam
from your busy kettle self

sufficient as a rhyming couplet.
You, my lovely always, on which I thread
each drawn breath, each yawn
a bead, dear one, an eye.

A tired woman with violet moons
hanging from her eyes, skin
blanched sleepless attracts
lovers who calculate that languor

inclines her to the horizontal.
Hard, darling, to wake clutching
a jumping knot of arteries, sky varicose
and hoarse with pigeon. Aah, baby

turning her pursed dawn face this way,
that. Sunflower on the stalk, eyes
heliotropic. The pain
is back, a crack covered in

expertly with prepositions. Spring
rains dash cherry blossom, but desire
blooms metaphorically
in the haiku of the young. I cannot

of course, speak for the middle-aged.
Called her a hybrid strain
"turn her to the light once a week"
he said. Let me explain

it is posture not pain keeps me
vertical. The horizon no nearer today
than yesterday, a sun directly overhead,
neither judicious nor merciful.

La Madonna parts her hair, through
root and cuticle, claws
the bird with shocked eyes.
Will this turn out to be the long

narrative poem about the mother,
dead but insomniac
by habit? She paces the rooms
in her loose flowing skin, rolls

her wrists back at the cuff. Snip-snip,
two eyelids fall out of the dark. She
will never sleep again. Hush li'l bird,
fly away dropping baby v's. She

wants to sleep curled like a comma
between heroic couplets. The pain
is back, the hairline crack, fish
hook through the gills reeling

that mackerel tongue. Hard, darling,
to come to this place, the years
crossed like wings over wet
language flaring in the throat,

a draught of poison to agitate
the follicles. And memory
forced like embalming fluid
through the body's cooling cavities.

Hey little you, little bird. Hey there.
Haven't spoken for awhile,
too busy with your stiff-legged
learning-to-walk, palms-braced self.

Huff-huff, each breath squeezed
in soft buds, the head on her thin
green nape. *Flâneur* baby stalking
Thomasina-next-door come to wriggle

her pouncing self in the poke and itch
of grass cut crew. Little walker, you
are all verb, all movement, all static
shooting from the comb's familiarity.

Only days since we taught you
to sleep. You crying in one room,
me in the other. Your father
running between us with a stopwatch

until morning cut its petals pink
and fresh as fingernails parted
from the flesh. Too fast, lovely one.
I am not charmed, have imitated

the tabby all my life, kept
my distance from the beauty
that waylays us: the kiss
against which all writing languishes.

Blue Lines

To turn his car
in directions I didn't, and bring
all those roads into the headlights?
"Someone has stayed in Stockholm"

Don Coles

There are places you can only get to by dying
or writing. There are places that cannot be paraphrased.
The sky curved behind windshield glass,
muffled pines, the scarred pelt of a mountain range,
reason in all its convex forms. In the place of words,
a trackless blue hum. Her life
tilting into misdemeanour, into memory.

This girl is never in one place for very long, she buttons
herself distractedly down the middle, smooths
gloves over callous knuckles. Away, away —

Begin by skidding on black ice. Fish-tailing across lanes,
she lands in a snowbank. Late fall, the world
creaking at its hinges. Behind her the mountains
click shut. For context, imagine birds blurred
silently on branches, a threadbare fall of snow
slurring the windshield. *Woke up dis mornin'*
sings car radio, *wit an artful acorn dread.*

◦◦◦

For context imagine a stalled car
or mind, jammed and ticking over
with the double-crossing blues. *Woke up*
in mourning, in mourning —

◦◦◦

If you study the coordinates you will
come to a place that has no double.

◦◦◦

Begin by going back. She drives headlong
into the mountains. They are too quick for her, parting
with oblique disdain, murmuring *sesame, sesame*. The highway
may well be an intrepid metaphor. Notice
how it moves in both directions at once, pausing
only to halve small towns like pumpkins, already seeded
on other maps.

All night before she leaves, snow purls
from a puckered sky. Little words fly to earth:
still, stall, stay. *Enough*, she whispers into a cupped hand,
so long (for so long now . . .) November
is not a time but a place.

W 117° 20' — W 115° 10'
N 52° 16' — N 50° 42'
(or thereabouts)

Yesterday or maybe later than that. She arrives,
slips into water. Since swimming is her alibi
for love or grief, the body's subtle fortitude, or any
two things spliced together without the lying word.

∽

Like the way words crackle and freeze
shuttling between meaning and its opposite.
Cool and burning, that girl in her *crisp* skin.

∽

Swimming and the line, the length. Languid
poems break through water: *a little, alive
always*. All this water of which she is a part,
apart — The highway roars open, she dives,
drives full into snow, fathoms awake. A wake
like a pale scribble on water.

∽

Does she shed, do the years shed her, does she
come to this place the past jangling in her pocket
like spare change, keys, a roll of film?
The opposite of memory is the name of her old lover
tattooed in small letters along an inner thigh. For context,
imagine light thinning to wind, the world tilting on its axis.
Watch the roots of her hair grow, the skin
on her heels flake away. The small of her back,
her nape, are characters in a black and white movie.
She stumbles, oh —

By the time you get this we will have spoken.

Before leaving she washes the kitchen floor,
waters plants. Forks in their narrow drawers
scribble scribble. A carving knife represses the memory of skin
crisping at its edges. Outside snow falls without emphasis
but with a certain syntactical rigour. She is persuaded
by snow, the metered despair blank as verse. Snow
like backstroke, another way to withdraw.

Memory: the compact fact of all she's lost
over the span of a day with serrated wings.
Rising early with the wind that precedes narrative,
chivvying leaves, cigarette butts, the imperfect future. Dying
in a small fall of light over the tightrope of noon. The wind,
I mean.

In the mountains again, shrugging into the present tense
from the parenthesis of memory like a sweater flung casually
over bowed shoulders. Saying here, and here. *Here*.
A corner of the hallway decants nostalgia, the sky
leaves blue rinse deposits on her palms.

Overcome by kindness or its opposite, her body
and its delicate limbs unstrung. A face appears
dismayed, through blue cleavage of water.
Every moment jumps from her mouth like a dying fish,
torn scales hanging from lips, her eyes. As she swims,
little cells unlock, open doors all over her body, her skin
a fine mesh of sieve and trawl. Is memory
what is preserved or what is lost? What I recall
are synonyms for blue: water and sky, the colour
of the eye turned inwards.

Outside these eyes, the mountain. There
is no verb for the mountain. Immovable except
when beckoning idiomatically to Mohammed.

this face, her dear face,
siphoned off from the past

In this poem someone has travelled from here to there.
Someone is revisiting old places, meeting herself half
way, the one who never left. She finds herself, for example,
caught like tulle in the branches of a tree, or flaring
briefly in the stairwell, the years folded awkwardly
across her shoulder blades.

Every ascension is lovely, even a matter of stairs.

All the sleepless nights between now and then,
a slough of weeks after the clocks fall backwards
into November, sky blue-veined as a breast.
She fled home in order to steal a word
that preserves sadness in its folds. Thinks often
of that sweetrotten place she departed
in the intervals between birds. The earth,
after all, is a habit not easy to break.

By the time you get this I will have left.

You scab-picker you, small face pinched
between winters. The tinsel in your eye
distracts magpies as you mumble the sky
smiling between the missing teeth your tongue
remembers. In this once lovely
and congenial world we are in constant danger
of immortality.

How to get home: fly into the sun
for a day and a night. Then follow
the girl declining her tense double
down a street too narrow for company.

Why are words always turning into birds
falling through turbulence, opening
into draft and blur? What is a word?
A stroke, a wing, a pigeon, a white dove,
a breast. She is fading as I write,
every other word recognizable only
in the path of its flight. Perhaps, after all,
there is no polite way to withdraw
from the privilege of the first person.

All the sleepless nights between here and there, like
a hand of solitaire face down on worn baize, like
swimming the blues, throwing indelible lines over cool
water. Like meeting yourself on a street you remember
never having taken.

Says she favours tattoos, impermanent
as the memory of these blue lines. Hey,
beautiful, throw me a line, she calls,
too low to hear. Every third word slightly
erased, as if blurred by a wet thumb. Always
known we are lost in a long poem, fragmented
to gloss memory, she says.
Nevertheless, she adds, treading water,
I am not as melancholy as I seem to be
when that complaint escapes me.

What is a word? Four letters lost in the mail.

Dreary dreary, quite contrary. An overexposed sky
tensing to brace the mountains. In the photograph,
a single frame, subliminal as loss, this moment
blurs. Light falls, recurs, recalls itself in the fine
cursive of fir and pine. The mountain is another word
for memory, what rises to the surface preserved
through amnesia, what blurs.

The journey back is twenty-four hours
flying straight into night. Is memory
what allows us to forget
appointments and faces, the words
to a song about the blues, blue
lines, blue eyes, blood roses breaking through
the ripe blue skin?

Or else I am who is here, the other girl only
a matter of mind over mirror. If I called her ghost,
she would take on entirely too much substance,
the one who never left, the adjective who keeps my place
in the sentence.

⁂

The problem with swimming is how to remain
on the surface. Go too deep, reader, and you drown.
For the sake of the swimmer, let us agree to forsake
all depth metaphors.

⁂

(Preserve this by forgetting it,
immediately.)

⁂

Because we're so awkward, you might assume
we are lovers. The way to tell us apart:
one of us fades, the other dissolves in salt.
One of us is melancholy as snow on the day
you leave the mountains for good. The other only leaves
for bad, her heart creaking ajar in the dark,
neither mournful nor nostalgic. Both are lost
& found, borrowed & lent, saved, spent. Neither
is optimistic enough to believe in memory
rising to the surface like a Halloween pumpkin.

She, the irreplaceable, the one who refuses her place,
the guarantor of a promise I did not make.

When she leaves, she leaves
something behind,
frequently herself.

Why not kill me, she demands wearily,
once and for all?
What proves, I reply, I've not
done so and more than once?

A soft-toothed sound, a *blur*.
A word written and erased
once too often.

When she swims she forgets home, forgets
pity and terror, the tragic enterprise and all joys
not entirely vicious. Her hands open, empty
as Ophelia's hands were empty. This
is how to preserve memory: in shale like a fossil,
in vinegar like plums, in amber like a fly, in salt
like meat, like snow, in camphor like underwear,
under glass, behind the arras, packed
in ice. Or misfiled in a brown manila envelope
like a poem.

By the time you get this we will be together again.

Halloween, kids dump pumpkins into the pool
demonstrating that forgetfulness is the first tense
goad to memory, etc. Do all nouns
float? Pumpkins and potatoes, pianos. The bitter
and playful eggplant?

One of us draws close to the window, hoping
to catch daylight before it is earthed in pines.
One of us steps demurely into water, proving
her high disdain for what pulls us under: various
blues, blurred and slovenly love, the body's
saline tides. One of us breaks light open
with a stone, one of us searches
without conviction for her metonymic shadow.
Imagine two figures caught in a doorway
one coming, one going, and nothing
to choose between your punctual body,
my tardy grin.

An amended list of amnesias and how to preserve them: hair
in lockets, flowers between books, photographs behind glass.
The fingerbones of dilatory saints in reliquaries. The word
reliquary in the dictionary. The heart, that hot & sensual organ,
through exercise, a little red wine; the soul through good deeds
and bad. As for the dead, try rosemary. That's for remembrance.

☙

I know no other definition of what is hard than this, reader,
this: rising up to the surface, the promiscuous self-disclosure
of sunlight.

☙

By the time you get these blue lines I will be drowning in revisions.

☙

Scent of a girl (spirited) in a stairwell (empty)
air turning madder in her wake. Somewhere
else, shoes capsized beneath a chair.
There are moments of connection, the wound
of separateness healed. There are moments like puberty,
teetering.

In the end I am only interested in what cannot be preserved. Turn the page.

Narrow groove of skin between nose and lip
a column of forgetfulness where officious angels
with their punctual thumbs mark the soul's crisp
passage from here to there, unconvinced
by arguments in favour of reason, or memory
inexact as correspondence. But this double life, how
to live split down the middle, ah my chevalier?

The first hour is a deep breath, a blue line flung
over the possibility of suspension. She arcs a slow
crescent, water streaming from her flanks, arms in perfect
parenthesis about the mind's imperfect emptiness. Next,
a small tree grows in the space between her lungs,
throws out branches and leaves, steals air. After this
all is wild regret tempered by time cropped
into units of breath. The past hissing through her veins
in indigo spurts.

      water flows through
      her body a sleek
      & rhythmic conduit
      returning like to like

If there is a relation between memory and backstroke
it is that both suppose an extenuation of the subject
in another medium. Waters break above her and the sky, blue
as counterfeit blood.

⊷

Turning, she returned to check the oven, proving
that small dear thing neglected in some other life
haunts her still. To go back without direction, keys, without
the consolation of grief, gloves, etc. Only memory, pallid
as the arms of that girl writing her blue lines, including me
at the bottom of her letter, a reluctant postscript.

⊷

Pray, love.

⊷

She cannot age, she cannot die. She sidles up to me
at street corners to ask for direction, harangues me
from empty doorways. Late at night my windows sing
let me in let me —. In the morning pebbles on my pillow
mark remembrance at an open grave. Her symbolism
impeccable: *only an honest woman admits she's a good
liar*. She will always inhabit this place, her body shot
with instinct, rustling in its sleeves. Her mouth a wound,
her salty pleas.

— having fallen already, having become attached to poverty
of expression, having grown immune to verbs. Having grown
sleek gills behind my ears, having tracked the girl
with the punctuation mark tattooed above her mouth. Having
felt my heart quicken in the dark, neither slant nor enchanted.
Having made my peace with arrhythmia, having learnt that faith
is an epidermal affair, having gathered the shards
of my broken reserve, having put myself entirely
at grief's disposal —

I give up these words easily, they are easy
to give up, like changing currency before
a border: the cursive line between mountain
and sky, say, as perfect a mismatch as any
made in heaven.

The risk of forgetting, momentarily, our debt
to gravity: time's slow release
a capsule in the blood. Every moment
recognizable only in the shadow cast
by the imperfect past, perfectly tensed
to catch on sorrow and sprocket. Like the way
a drowning girl unspools in the water, the end
of the film flapping across her wet cheek.

Length by opulent length, following her truant breath
to the other side.
       Afloat. One of those indivisible words
even half of which
       is wholly buoyant. In her wake,
a dissolving sentence: *this problem with the line
break, where to end and how to say
good-bye.* One hand reaches out, touches
tiled wall —

Trawling: A Biography of the River

In commemoration of the brief but not uneventful hyphen

between the birth of Heraclitus in 535 BC

and the great Winnipeg flood of 1997.

The river is the object of our surveillance, our wary red-eyed scrutiny. Into its billows engineers drop weights and measures. The day of the crest is moved forward bird by bird. Chess pieces all over the city stand on bridges watching the river rise. The backs of their heads, crossed shoulder blades expressive of waiting, breath held.

Knights, bishops, tilting pawns — their undefended napes, how brave and pointless!

Kitchen staff at a riverside café smoke and genuflect. Some controversy, it seems, about the correct gesture. Right over left, up and down, or left over right? The air is a sponge, a heel of bread sopping light from the bowl of the sky.

So far no one has referred to the river by the female pronoun. It is only a matter of time.

A city perforated along the banks of rivers, a city that swallows itself, periodically, disastrously. A city of floods and fevers, this old flat weary prairie town.

Every moment is already past, spent. We cannot step into the same river twice. Women, schoolchildren in boots and work gloves pass sandbags hand to hand. They do not step into the river at all on account of prudence rather than philosophy.

Is it possible, enquires perverse Cratylus, to step even once into the same river?

Splashed across the headlines his words provoke a *flood* of letters to the editor. We step and do not step into the same river, writes Hukluk of Ste. Anne, MB., we are and are not. Alternately, quibbles "Muddy Waters," if what we mean by "river" is the flux of existence then we are always and never in the same river. At some point all analogies break down, prevaricates H. Shipley (Mrs.). That is not the point, replies Zeno Meisner of Steinbach, snappish with the effort of partitioning his argument.

In editorials exasperation chases relief across six inch columns, the latter moving over the surface like the colours in an oilslick.

Meanwhile, all across the city, homeowners are searching out back-up valves for their sewers, bracing themselves for that abject moment when what is hidden

rises.

The river has turned malign, boiling along its edges as if feverish. Colour of black tea or bile. Sucks and pulls at its banks, an animal gnawing itself free from a trap. An old man pulling at his iodine lips, sipping tea through a sugar cube.

There is no avoiding personification when it comes to the river.

The river is famished, greedy, angry because no one loves it, starving for love. Or, the river is incontinent, abundant, the river unclasps its thighs, thundering. Too much water has been released, too much strength is needed for reticence. Too many words are required to sop it up, to travel backwards into water as wine into forgetfulness.

Bitten-down lips, wet eyes, how do you fight a river? Address the troops, identify the enemy. Say, the enemy is approaching, the enemy never sleeps.

The old city flaps in the scaffolding of evening. Headless, a woman hurries away beneath her umbrella. Somewhere in the sky a switch is thrown, an orange bigger than a sun rolls west.

Heraclitus, the engineer, rolls the iron hoops of his mind about the wooden barrel of his problem. As he ponders, his soul settles deep in his body, sediment.

How to hold back water, how to hold water within? The bladder, perhaps, the mouth. Dashes off a fleet sketch: down to the banks of the Red in relays, citizens like thirsty cattle. Put reluctant mouths to the river's lip.

Heraclitus' eyes are green as the word damp. He orders another glass of absinthe to fondle his heart, returns to his graph. The waitress is weary, tendrils back of the neck damp and intimate, her eyelids thin as grapeskin. She wants to go home, put her bed on cinder blocks, but the last customer gazes into his cloudy lees, cries out, strikes a curt temple with the flat of his hand.

What did she say?

Upright, straddling his pain. On his shoulder a tame raven named Horace, account of his hoarse voice. Heraclitus holds his pencil at arm's length, measures the distance between bridges, the depth of the crest. (The width between her eyes.) The waitress turns away snagging fingers through the rivulets of her hair, *oh*—

What did she say to provoke such a kiss?

Almost nothing is known of Heraclitus' life before the flood. Afterwards, the details are anecdotal, unreliable. But a photograph exists, stippled newsprint, pointillist river in the foreground. Wind-whipped body, bending from the waist like a reed. Tall, some would say too. All that enhanced meat he ate as a boy, prepared without love or seasoning!

Who knows, he is reported as musing in later life, what you get with your slice of beef. (This is neither insignificant nor the reason for everything.)

No commentary accompanies the photograph. As always, the camera is speechless. Above his head the Provencher bridge slumps in the middle, dragging its shallow belly through the mud.

Consider the belated problem of synchronicity: if the bridge tumbled into the river would different waters flow through once? Twice?

The bridge drags itself on its belly through mud as if it knows that whatever lives lives by the destruction of its opposite. In the city a man waits. The waters cut him, like the bridge, in half.

Six men have borne the name Heraclitus. The first a philosopher, a riddler, an obscurist surpassing all others in arrogance and disdain. Eyes wet as yolk, he disjointed thought as if it were a roast. Known as Heraclitus the cuckoo-voiced, he delighted in obscuring the footsteps of his reasoning as if to say: this is a peculiar time for reverie and I am unskilled at the plot, even of my own life. He also compared *hubris* to a blazing fire in need of extinguishing, and to this end submerged himself in a passing river.

All else proceeds from there.

Six men have borne the name Heraclitus, the second was a lyric poet who, forgetting his debt to gravity, took flight. Beneath him the city writhed in neon, and children, their small bones laid flat as wings, pursued him as if he were a kite. The third, an elegiac poet from Halicarnassus, is best known for the art he achieved in dying. *They told me, Heraclitus,* wept Callimachus, *they told me you were dead.*

Callimachus, strapping words to the grief his life was bound to like a wheel.

The fourth, native of Lesbos, wrote the definitive history of Macedonia and the fifth was a cithara-player who later became a jester, comedy being easier than fingering. (Met at the old *Cheque, Mate!* Heraclitus spilling his wineskin into the lap of Heraclitus, trying to mop him dry.)

Of the sixth Heraclitus three things are known: he tried to save a town from drowning, he wore his pet raven like an epaulet. He was peripheral and always sodden.

Oh, four things: once he made a hole in the world, now he can't pinch it closed.

Whether he ever said, in so many words, "you can't step twice into the same river," is widely disputed.

Logs thrash upstream grinding water between spiteful flanks. The skulls of cats, small birds, evil thoughts, bob upon the surface of the river, a contagion of blood and slow bone.

Along the banks, spindles of driftwood daub mud in colours that, one suspects, can only be named underwater, if at all. A city that smells of bandages or would if anyone were impolite enough to mention it.

A chain is only as strong as its weakest link, a city councillor announces with an air of originality, his arm around the sloped shoulders of strangers. All about him the city jangles in chains. New-minted as the reflection of the sun on water, his words ring like the bells of St. Boniface Cathedral.

Ding-dong, the sandbaggers flex rhythmically as a bracelet flashing in the sun. From arm to braced arm, as if handing over a loaf of newborn bread, an infant.

This city of volunteers, of lovingkindness. Along river banks, the carcasses of cattle and good deeds slump past.

Generations choking in his throat Heraclitus, the engineer, sneezes once for sorrow, twice for joy. Horace-on-the-shoulder cocks his head at an elderly couple on a bridge. With gothic poise, they watch the river rise. The long calcified haul has not exhausted them, nor yet the hard ethic of bone and breath. Still, the inching water refutes Archimedean logic, reminds that blood also rises the better to fall and, falling, drags the body like a tide.

On a napkin Heraclitus sketches furiously. Pulleys and locks, from tangles of spindrift darkening beneath water he models a dam, a ditch. The café fills with wreaths of faces, slow lassoes of smoke.

"And did you know, things are much worse than they're telling us, *much*."

In rapid succession a waitress sneezes five times for silver, six for gold. Flood's done nothing to tamp down the lilacs this year! Convulsed, the whole city sneezes, *achew!* in unison.

Seven for a secret can never be told mumbles Horace, beak ratcheting a wing.

Into his mouth Heraclitus pitches a forkful of honey and ashes. (Call it desire, if that is not too strong a word for pastry.)

Caw, croaks Horace, the relish of his love turning bitter in the maw.

Heraclitus sleeps, falling boneless through the layers of the city: shredded wind, water, the winding sheets of the dead.

A voice, breaking on the word *cloister*, chimes. Bells through the rising waters ring, *ring* and, ringing, rattle the soul's wrought cage.

Beneath the dusty awning of a café Heraclitus reads from the green rectangle of his Michelin. *Riverun past the ghosts dancing on Riel's grave.* Grass in the afternoon, a harp the wind misuses.

Out west, people give directions as if you've lived here all your life. Turn left at the Salisbury House, they say. Just after the flowering Dogwood.

Before him, immense and segmented, the Cathedral. White as sugar as bone as lace, white as the magnesium flash. As the little oblong of paper before the Polaroid begins to appear.

Pale stone and devotion, ringing.

Easy enough to say *grace* on a day when the sun shines
unexpectedly between slanted eaves, sloping years.

Perhaps none of this is true, perhaps none of this occurred:

cloister   sun   dogwood   bone
grass   wind   water   lace
bell   sugar   river   stone
voice   shine   breaking   grace

Perhaps none of this.

Instead: coffee like baggy brown corduroy. A morning already crimped
at the edges.

At the Forks a marketer chooses fish from a tangle of goldleaf and scale, her raw
hands. A translucent sole weighed between slippery palms, slap slap.

The listeners who call into 99.9, Winnipeg's Lite Rock Station, all request the same song.
Over the radio slow spaces open, close, wind swinging sound waves into parabola and
sine curve. This goes out to all you flood victims, this—

Colours blow across the fish counter, gilt, pastel, scale, zinc.
Gut, slit, fishblood, stink.

A waitress pulls the damp strands of hair off the back of her neck.

In cupboards wire hangers clatter, shirts dream of breasts and a pair of stockings
begins to run.

A sleek American (plush, almost up*hol*stered) lounges
in Departures, yells "queen to pawn seven!" into his cell phone.

What the river carries, explains the CBC announcer over the evening news, is sentiment. Excuse me, he corrects himself, I mean sediment.

A philosopher (emeritus) turns to his wife: do you want tomatoes with your supper? Darling, I don't like tomatoes, she replies. You should, he says.
They have had this conversation every night for the past ten years.

The boy with the raven bristling from his shoulder decides to do away with himself. Might as well dispose of it all! Folds himself into a blue-box for pick-up come morning. He fails to notice the smell of cigarettes outdoors, little notes of crooked jazz. (Air soft as pubic hair, the aureoles around street lights.)

Behind his back the river roars by, lugging its thick scum of sentiment.
Nostalgie de la boue, as they say down in St. Boniface, a yearning
for mud.

After his lover departed, first fastidiously separating his collected library of the works of Sigmund Freud from their rainbow covers, Heraclitus retired to the temple of Artemis where he was often to be found playing dice with the children.

Love was the river that crested in him, then broke. Mornings, he lay between the sheets feeling the weight of water, the lip of the cup against his own.

Can you create drought from a deluge? he asks the children, one hand to his waterlogged heart. Of course the children do not understand him, no one does. His trenchant sayings remain impenetrable, although more lucid, it must be admitted, than the commentaries penned in his name.

Mumbling with lips warm from sleep for the cool lip of the cup, wondering if metonymy is the only sure way to bring the lover back home. Such violence!

Theophrastus says melancholia caused him to write with dispatch, as if to catch wingèd thought before it burnt away at the edges.

(No, that is not why he began to laugh and couldn't stop and had to be shaken lightly, then harder, until his head bent far as it would go on the fulcrum of his spine.)

Ah, soft-boiled youth welling slowly. Rising to the declivity of a spoon rapped staccato, tut-tut-tut against the cup.

It is better, says Heraclitus, his face expressionless as a clock without hands, to conceal ignorance.

Let me tell you a story. Once he tried to draw a cell lanced from the inside of his mouth. Around him, school mates peered through microscopes, sketched plasma and membrane, compact cell walls. Gingerly and with august concentration, Heraclitus produced a line drawing of his left eye, all he could glimpse through convex glass. Crikey, exclaimed the biology master, Strikes me there's an egotism at work here!

Ah swift-wingèd youth, the world is, was, and ever will be full of wonder.

Afterwards, a temptation to renounce machinery, to relate how watches never kept time on his wrist. Slow blood ticking time subtly awry.

Or: consider the word *wonder* which carries implications of breathlessness and treachery. Lovers consigned to dust and golden lads tarnishing as we breathe.

How everything turns away, quite leisurely, from the disaster.

Prairie light grainy as newsprint. River banks speckled with ground bone, the memory of pulped creatures crawling from discarded shells.

In the foreground, a river raging with kleptomaniac desire.

(The river, says Aristotle consulting an appendix in *The Interpretation of Dreams*, is one of the great structural metaphors for humanity. The other, of course, is the garden. But that's another story.)

Why, the desire to steal a little something from what won't be missed, of course. A white knight, a smoked olive, the teaspoon from an airline meal (the photo he took when she wasn't looking). In the case of the river, a pair of engineer's thighs (braced) cantilevering off the Provencher bridge.

The city, through a sudden crook of elbow, startles.

It was spring when Heraclitus fell. An air of undismayed hopefulness. Biting down hard as if on a champagne cork jammed in his mouth.

A raven winching overhead, wings burning, *they told me Heraclitus, they told me you were dead—*

Prairie light falls precise as a shutter closing on an eye open to the possibility of introspection. Out here we rely on the gathered light of the dead to reflect something of our hopes and grief. To rescue insignificant moments from obscurity. (Like the woman, *imagine*, who photographed the end-of-flood fireworks with a flashbulb!)

How everything turns away.

—————— ⟳ ——————

They told me Heraclitus, they told me you were dead,
They brought me bitter news to hear and bitter tears to shed.
I wept as I remembered how often you and I
Had tired the sun with talking and sent him down the sky.

Callimachus

(280-245 BC)

Kiss by the Hôtel de Ville, 1950,
and Other Kisses Various

To look through the viewfinder and disappear.
To lose a mouth in translation, to find
an eye for the gap between earth and sky, the horizon's
aperture contracting to sunrise or set, the landscape's
failure to escape.

⸎

Commuters outside the Hôtel de Ville. Blurred imprints
on a tilting street prove what we forget: the earth's
hesitation, the sun's regret. Two figures joined at the lip's seam,
an embrace taken in stride. The fortuitous moment
between the kiss and its adjective.

⸎

Everyone recognizes that photo by Doisneau, anyone can buy
cheap postcards at a news stand. The reproduction's thin slice
cut from the world, vivid as processed cheese. *Again,* she whispers.

He bends to the perfect repetition of her mouth.

Photographic plates need time to absorb light, lovers
growing into their embrace, coinciding briefly
during the long exposure.

⤙⤚

Her face like Venetian glass, blown from his curved lips.

⤙⤚

Or: *sticky,* she feels caught. As if she has mislaid her handkerchief
or her virtue. Both fingered, impossibly (fingered)
by strangers.

Ah, and what do objects included in the frame
have in common besides proximity? One
threadbare gesture pared from intention, one
small gleam between lid and lash. Our eyes
thinned to filament: *more light more light*.

❧

The photographer of chance meetings and delayed appointments,
Doisneau may be compared to a thief at the scene of the crime.
Of course he would deny loitering. Every moment is crisp with guilt,
he might have protested, every photograph an occasion
for giving, for getting. For bearing the past forward
into what *ever* is for.

❧

Or: her pale skin supple as vellum, the pliant wax
of her lips, his peremptory seal. The kiss
an impartial letter, the only intermediary between the image
and its repetition.

The photographer on one knee before the double-bladed moment
slicing itself from all possible kisses past and to come.

❧

An image of the face coinciding with an image of the duration of the face.

❧

What is lost in the inexact translation from close-up to still-life?

> Warmth of mouth passed
> between lips, a taut
> mouthful of air, cup-shaped.

Think of all the pictures he did not take, all the moments
not "rescued" from obscurity. *Again,* she whispers, forever panting, forever
young, this narrow intersection of stone, breath, crooked light, and time
cheated of its proper corruption.

❧

An image flutters like dark moth
against light-sensitive paper. In this photograph
they are joined at the syllable
of the mouth, their lips glued
via the fixity of bromide.

❧

Eyes open to watch pleasure radiate
on his face like the spokes of a wheel, ripples
on a lake disturbed by something hard
and densely compacted, falling.

A stone or a kiss.

Click, the sound of an image cleated into place.

⚮

Every casual glance an act of perverse faithfulness, turning
fragment into jigsaw. (And all that this implies of light
moving to the surface of fugitive things, dissolving,
for example, on skin.)

⚮

Click. The kiss tumbling in its lock.

A Fall Between Kisses

This is a story about falling again (thought I
got it out of my system). Was standing on the edge
of a hole someone dug for some reason. Or:
I was standing on the edge of reason. For
some reason I fell in, hit my head on, say, a rock.
Three weeks later I fell in love with a photographer, fell
hard. (So here I am again, once around the world and back.)
Wouldn't mention it except for the dying fall linking
both stories and the feeling each time of gravity
sewn into the soles of my shoes.

What does the camera lie about? Light divided by time.
A kiss cropped between truth and reproduction (or twenty-four kisses
on a contact sheet, opening and closing with sticky wings).
His elongated jawbone, *her* strain of rareness. The shunt
of narrow streets through slipshod feet.
A kiss (let's try this again) perforated like a postage stamp
along international timelines. The long
shallow bones of her pelvis. A kiss (one last time) lured
to the surface of emulsified paper, fluttering in tight circles
on one wing.

It is well to remember, he told them,
that the camera adds at least five pounds
to the naked kiss.

The ideal photographer is the opposite of the lover. With either, beauty
waylays us. We have the impression that the picture (much like the kiss)
has been stolen rather than taken. *Click,* slant light catches on sprocket,

their faces spool into the undeveloped darkness of a few useful objects jangling in a pocket.

Falling, Burning

I undressed quickly (surreptitiously) my nipples
pointed politely away, excuse me excuse me.
The photographer made me pivot, snatched
hasty clips of nape, cleft, heel. All the places
without eyes, all the monosyllabic blind spots.

I was (I confess) moved by the thought
of those bitter hopeful eyes gazing
upon the eyeless Gaza of my back.

The photographer forced a retractable lens
down my throat, between my thighs (our glances
clasping and un) to demonstrate a concern
with the root, the deep follicle, the cuticle of things.
With digital precision winter opened inside me
radiating from my centre.

Years later, the woman at the Hôtel de Ville will step forward. *Mais oui*, she will say, actors not lovers. We kissed all day under his exacting eye, hold, then release, *hold*. After that I lost my appetite, each new affair awkwardly choreographed, unobserved. No impertinent flash of light to recall where an embrace ended and I, again, began.

❧

A photograph, the bright pause we all get to at the same time.

❧

Of course we are disappointed, cheated, in fact. The question of authenticity aside, where is the compulsion now to seek the precise angle of the jaw where accident tautens to intention? The kiss flying into the future tense before it has properly dried.

After the Fall

Say cheese, he said, say please.
With digital precision winter opened inside me
radiating from my centre. Wider, he said
(rummaging), smile for the camera.

Apropos of honey, he remarked,
I should like to taste the hollow at your throat.
Actually, I replied, I am neither as sweet nor as sticky
as I appear. Cookie-wise I tend to crumble
(but that's the way). Except, of course, for the arch
of my left foot which has been rubbed repeatedly
against the lips of the pious.

He centred me between tripod hands,
                a view splayed, dis
played across the austerity of white walls, stiletto ideals.
All my doors gaped at once.
                    And winter,
as I have already indicated, swung wide.

The kiss is as good a way as any of providing an excuse for lapses
of memory, of taste, a reason to close the argument or the eyes. He rarely
lowered the camera, didn't want to miss anything. The stutter
of film across shutter only another way to say I was here here here.

༒

I leave out altogether the problem of interpretation.
On this point, alone, no misunderstanding is possible.

༒

She reminded him that Flaubert believed every photograph
rubbed away a thin layer of skin. He replied, the photographer
as voyeur is a metaphor that offers a certain *frisson*
but one that need not concern our good selves.
                              Her skin is not transparent
not yet. It will take years and the saw-toothed battlements
of her clavicles (poking through) to believe in bone again,
flesh that need not resolve to adieu and breasts,
sundering careful neck buttons, spoiling the line of shirtwaists.

His hectoring glance smeared
across glossy prints
like a palm on glass or lipstick on the rim of a cup.
Each photograph an imprint of the gaze, each
peach   moth   kiss   dusting the surface
for fingertips, lips, for teeth marks, a wing.

Those sad afternoons when we stumbled
from the dark studio, yawning
into dilatory light, the long exposure.
Empty, untempted.

My skin is not opaque, not yet, she said. Still,
you can no longer glimpse the blood flow
below the surface. For contrast
(if you look very carefully) an old kiss
at Hôtel de Ville, 1950 or thereabouts,
after which my life fell steeply into before

and outside. Much like your mouth, his glance,
this page.

Tempestuous

Prospero: I have done nothing but in care of thee,
Of thee, my dear one; thee, my daughter.

At an odd angle of the island, the deposed Duke of Milan turns to his daughter. She is already a little threadbare with obedience, but fresh, young, open-throated. Her silence is not reticence but a small habit she cultivates: a knot in the handkerchief, a stone in the shoe. She sleeps with great concentration, agitating the night like a bellows to her restless breath. Perhaps she is dreaming of the lover who will tear open her sleep like an envelope and climb inside. In the morning her sheets are uncharacteristically rumpled, an open letter.

Her father, an unrequited reader, takes sorry note of his daughter's condition. Come walk with me a little way into the trees, he says, thinking to cure her *ennui* in a brisk wind.

Such a dreary day, the sky hanging in loose folds from trees like tent poles, and he is weary of scraping small leavings from the bottom of his mind with a dull knife. *I have done nothing* — the wind empties all words from his mouth, winnows her body to a reed. They are a pencil sketch, then a pair of graphite lines on the horizon.

Listen, he is not a man I am inclined to admire, what with his sibilant spells, his capital Art. Prosperous, he commands slaves and spirits, the whole unrepentant island and one pale, blue-veined daughter slightly erased about the temples by his curt regard. Look, already she has begun to unravel from the world, her fingertips blank. Her palms on cold glass leave no print. But when he turns to her, his father's arms fallow, and cries *my dear one, my daughter*, I am, I confess, moved.

Times like this I forgive his carnivorous mind, the cool undertow of his pity. Imagine the loose skin at his clavicles, his empty father's heart swinging all night on its latch. At dawn he bends over his sleeping daughter, straining to hear the itinerant breath that has begun to unhitch from the world as she sleeps.

Prospero: Young Ferdinand, — whom they suppose is drown'd, —

What we learn from these pages is how to stay afloat. Everyone else drowns. A father in his fathoms, a monster in his cups. Like pearls in wine, a son's pale flesh. Perdition in the angle of a neck, the bend of a wrist, the crook of a tree. As: Ferdinand, his heart sluiced open, suddenly and without impediment throws himself into her long surmise. As: Prospero, taking tea under a Ginkgo tree, floods the island with his strange imports, pound cake and bone china, a thirsty Georgian teapot.

He turns to Caliban. *Do have a Fig Newton, my boy.*

Even the books that have kept this place buoyant through shipwreck and patrimony are tilted into the sea at the end. By a man who has peeled himself thin as paper, by a man with a face like a book slammed shut.

Up on high ground, Miranda is bored, begins to unpick the landscape from her embroidery frame. Already the sky is pulling loose from the horizon, the leaves are fooled into an imaginary Fall. If you want to stay afloat, watch Miranda.

As light as the sponge cake her father orders for his morning tea, she rises above the island, her perfectly arched feet grazing the tilted pines. Tremulous stuff of indecorous dreams, she permits herself to be given away too easily. Or else too easily gives way.

No matter who else drowns on this equivocal shore, Miranda never even gets her feet wet.

| Prospero: | *What ho! slave! Caliban!* |
| | *Thou earth, thou! speak.* |

My body was the dark integument between memory and forgetfulness. You turned my skin into an embroidered coat, a reversible language. *You,* hypocrite lecteur, when you were done with me there was nothing I could not quote.

I found you bent over a map of the island, tracing a red arrow with one imperious forefinger: *you are here.* The forest creaked open, thrusting mushroom and moss into slow-veined air but there was no escaping your intention.

The first word you gave me was father.

We began with the trees: you taught me the longing in Pine, the hands in Palm, the sharp retort of Poplar. Father, you named the world out of all recognition, each word a pendulum in my uncertain blood, my mouth ajar, smoking. Always in the imperative mood, you'd point to this stone, that star, setting language ticking through my bones like a metronome.

Repetez, repetez! the stylus in your throat catching at the glottal click of memory on cartilage.

You pushed me through the narrow hinges of the world until the island faded behind a tapestry of unicorn and fruit. And I, left to thrust empty sleeves through the arras, groping for horn, snout, hoof. The word *Miranda* torn linen in my hands.

You for whom the animals flared rampant, the forest bending to your deep shield escutcheoned. Words struck to flint with mortal joy, father, you taught me the distances in your name.

Acknowledgements

The image of the red Queen of Spades in *A Year of Birds* is a reference to Erin Mouré's discussion of memory paradigms in an interview included in *West Coast Line* (Fall 1993).

The epigraph to *Blue Lines* is from Don Coles's poem "Someone has stayed in Stockholm" in *Forests of the Medieval World*.

The fragment by Callimachus is after the translation by W.J. Cory in *Ionica*.

I am very grateful for the support of the Banff Writer's Studio and the Canada Council for the Arts.

Thank you to Stan Dragland who took each of these poems by the scruff and shook 'em out, and grateful thanks to Maureen Harris and Kitty Lewis. And to Mark Libin, my own particular "without whom."

Biography

Méira Cook lives and writes in Winnipeg. She has published two previous collections of poetry, *A Fine Grammar of Bones* (Turnstone Press, 1993) and *Toward a Catalogue of Falling* (Brick Books, 1996), as well as a chapbook, *the ruby garrote* (disOrientations chapbooks, 1994). Her first novel, *The Blood Girls* (NeWest and Overlook Press), was published in 1998. *Taking the Waters* (Stacatto Chapbooks, 1995) is a fictional exploration of Freud's "Dora" case history.